WEBWIZARDRY SERIES

Dominating HTML Essentials and Beyond

Web Maverick

CONTENTS

CONTENTS

SEMANTIC HTML

Introduction:

"Welcome to the ultimate guide on Semantic HTML! Whether you're a beginner diving into web development or a seasoned coder looking to enhance your skills, this book is your roadmap to mastering the art of Semantic HTML. Join us on this journey as we unravel the secrets behind five crucial elements: Header, Nav, Article, Section, and Footer."

If you're reading this, you're probably familiar with HTML and its purpose in web development. HTML is the backbone of the internet, and Semantic HTML is the foundation of a well-structured website. So, what is Semantic HTML, and why is it so important?

Put simply, Semantic HTML is a way of writing HTML that focuses on the meaning of the content rather than its appearance. It's about using the right HTML tags to convey the purpose of the content to both search engines and humans. By doing so, you're not only making your website more accessible to people with disabilities, but you're also improving its visibility in search engine results.

Now, let's dive into the five crucial elements of Semantic HTML that we mentioned earlier:

Header: The header tag is used to define the introductory content of a page or section. It typically includes a logo, navigation menu, and other important information about the website.

Nav: The nav tag is used to define a set of navigation links. These links typically lead to other pages within the website or external sources.

Article: The article tag is used to define a self-contained piece of content that could stand alone on the web. This could be a blog post, news article, or any other content that is independent from the rest of the page.

Section: The section tag is used to define a group of related content. This can be used to organize content within an article, or to divide a page into different sections.

Footer: The footer tag is used to define the closing content of a page or section. It typically includes copyright information, social media links, and other important information.

By using these five crucial elements of Semantic HTML, you can create a well-structured and accessible website that is optimized for both search engines and humans. So, whether you're a beginner or a seasoned coder, mastering the art of Semantic HTML is a must for any web developer looking to create a successful website.

Understanding Semantic HTML:

"Let's kick things off by demystifying Semantic HTML. In this chapter, we'll explore the importance of semantic elements in web development, unraveling the benefits they bring to the table. Get ready to transform your code into a well-structured, accessible, and SEO-friendly masterpiece."

Semantic HTML is an essential aspect of web development that helps web developers create well-structured, accessible, and SEO friendly web pages. To achieve this, web developers use semantic elements that accurately describe the content of a web page. Here are some benefits of semantic HTML:

Improved accessibility: Semantic HTML helps to make web pages more accessible to users with disabilities. This is because these elements provide additional information to assistive technologies about the content of a web page, making it easier for users to navigate and understand the content.

Better SEO: Semantic HTML makes it easier for search engines to understand the content of a web page. This is because search engines rely on the HTML structure of a web page to determine its relevance to a particular search query.

Easier to maintain: Semantic HTML makes it easier to maintain a web page by providing a clear and consistent structure. This makes it easier for web developers to make changes to the content and structure of a web page without affecting its overall design.

In summary, using semantic HTML is crucial for creating well-structured, accessible, and SEO-friendly web pages. By using semantic elements, web developers can improve the overall user experience and make it easier for search engines to find and rank their web pages.

Semantic HTML plays a crucial role in web development by providing a meaningful structure to content. By using appropriate tags and elements, you can enhance both the clarity of your code and the understanding of your webpage's structure. This guide explores the best practices for utilizing semantic HTML elements and offers tips for maintaining clean and meaningful HTML code.

Understanding Semantic Elements (Header, Nav, Article, Section, Footer)

Semantic HTML is a way of writing HTML that emphasizes the meaning of the content rather than its presentation. Semantic HTML uses specific tags to describe the content of a web page, making it easier for search engines and screen readers to understand the structure of the page.

Here's a brief overview of some of the most commonly used semantic elements:

Header: The <header> element is used to define a header section for a document or a section. It usually tains a logo, navigation menu, and other introductory content.

Nav: The <nav> element is used to define a section of navigation links.

Article: The <article> element is used to define an independent, self-contained piece of content, such as a blog post or news article.

Section: The <section> element is used to define a section of related content.

Footer: The <footer> element is used to define a footer section for a document or a section. It usually contains copyright information, contact details, and other closing content.

Semantic HTML is not only beneficial for search engines and screen readers, but it also improves the accessibility and usability of a website. In addition to the elements mentioned in the previous content, here are some more examples of semantic HTML:

Main: The <main> element is used to define the main content area of a web page. It should contain the primary content of the page, excluding any header, footer, or sidebar elements.

Aside: The <aside> element is used to define a section of content that is indirectly related to the main content. It is often used for sidebars, callouts, or advertising.

Figure and Figcaption: The <figure> element is used to contain any media content such as images, videos, or audio. The <figcaption> element is used to provide a caption or description for the media content.

Time: The <time> element is used to define a specific date or time. It is particularly useful for publishing dates and times, event dates, or other time-related information.

Progress: The <progress> element is used to indicate the progress of a task, such as a download or upload. It can be used in conjunction with JavaScript to provide real-time progress updates.

By using semantic HTML, not only do you create a more accessible and user-friendly website, but you also improve the overall structure and organization of your content. This can lead to improved SEO and a better user experience for your visitors.

Here's an example of semantic HTML:

```html
<header>
 <h1>My Website</h1>
 <nav>
  <ul>
   <li><a href="#">Home</a></li>
   <li><a href="#">About</a></li>
   <li><a href="#">Contact</a></li>
  </ul>
 </nav>
</header>
<main>
 <article>
  <h2>Article Title</h2>
  <p>Article content goes here...</p>
 </article>
 <section>
  <h2>Section Title</h2>
  <p>Section content goes here...</p>
 </section>
 <aside>
  <h2>Aside Title</h2>
  <p>Aside content goes here...</p>
 </aside>
 <footer>
  <p>&copy; My Website 2023</p>
 </footer>
</main>
```

In this example, we have used semantic HTML elements to define the structure of a web page. The <header> element contains the site's logo and navigation menu, while the <main> element contains the main content of the page. The <article> element contains an independent piece of content, while the <section> element contains a section of related content. The <aside> element contains content that is related to the main content but not essential to it, and the <footer> element contains closing content such as copyright information.

In addition to using semantic HTML elements for page structure, there are other important considerations when creating a web page. Here are some tips to keep in mind:
Accessibility: Ensure that your web page can be used by people with disabilities. Use alt attributes for images, provide captions for videos, and make sure that your page is navigable using a keyboard.
Responsiveness: Your web page should be able to adapt to different screen sizes. Use media queries to adjust the layout and font sizes for smaller screens.

Performance: Optimize your web page so that it loads quickly. This can be achieved by minimizing the use of large images or videos, optimizing code, and using a content delivery network (CDN) to distribute content.
Search Engine Optimization (SEO): Use relevant keywords in your content and metadata to improve your page's visibility in search engine results.

Usability: Ensure that your web page is easy to use and navigate. Use clear and concise language, provide a logical layout, and use consistent styling throughout the page.

By keeping these considerations in mind, you can create a web page that is accessible, responsive, performant, optimized for search engines, and easy to use.

Choose Semantic Tags Wisely:
When structuring your HTML, opt for semantic tags that convey the meaning of the content they enclose. For instance, use `<article>` for self-contained content, `<nav>` for navigation links, `<header>` for introductory content, and `<footer>` for concluding information.

Semantic HTML tags are crucial for creating a well-structured website. They not only provide a clear structure to your content, but also help search engines understand the context of your web page. Here are some more tips for using semantic tags:

Use `<section>` to group related content together. This can be particularly useful for long articles or pages with multiple sections.

Use `<aside>` for content that is not directly related to the main content of the page, but is still relevant. This could include links to related articles or advertisements.
Use `<figure>` and `<figcaption>` to include images and captions. This can make your content more engaging and easier to understand.

Avoid using non-semantic tags like `<div>` or `<span>` for content that can be expressed using a semantic tag. This can make your HTML easier to understand and maintain.

Remember, the goal of using semantic HTML is to make your content more accessible and understandable to both humans and search engines. By using semantic tags appropriately, you can create a more structured and organized website that is easy to navigate and understand.

```
<article>
  <h2>Article Title</h2>
  <p>Article content goes here...</p>
```

```
</article>
<nav>
  <ul>
    <li><a href="#">Home</a></li>
    <li><a href="#">About</a></li>
    <!-- More navigation links -->
  </ul>
</nav>
<header>
  <h1>Website Title</h1>
  <p>Welcome to our website!</p>
</header>
<footer>
  <p>&copy; 2023 Your Website. All rights reserved.</p>
</footer>
```

Maintain Hierarchy with Headings:

Use heading tags (`<h1>` to `<h6>`) to create a clear hierarchy within your content. Ensure that each heading reflects the structure of the information it precedes.

Heading tags are a crucial component of any well-structured and organized content. They allow readers to quickly scan and understand the hierarchy of your content. Here are some tips for using heading tags effectively:

Use heading tags in order, starting with `<h1>` for the main title or header of your content. Subheadings should use `<h2>`, `<h3>`, `<h4>`, and so on, in descending order of importance. Avoid skipping heading levels. For example, don't use an `<h3>` tag directly after an `<h1>` tag without including an `<h2>` tag in between.

Use descriptive and concise headings that accurately reflect the content that follows. Avoid using generic headings like "Introduction" or "Conclusion."

Don't use heading tags for formatting purposes only. For example, don't use an `<h3>` tag in order to make a line of text larger or bolder.

Use a consistent style and formatting for your headings throughout your content. This helps to establish a clear visual hierarchy and makes your content easier to read and understand.
By following these guidelines, you can ensure that your headings are effective in communicating the structure and hierarchy of your content to your readers.

```
<h1>Main Heading</h1>
<p>Paragraph of text.</p>
<h2>Subheading</h2>
<p>Another paragraph of text.</p>
```

Maintaining a clear hierarchy with headings is a crucial aspect of creating well-structured and accessible web content. Headings not only help in organizing information but also provide a semantic structure for both users and search engines. Let's elaborate on the importance and usage of heading tags:

Headings provide a clear hierarchy of information: By using different heading levels, you can create a clear structure for your content. This enables readers to skim the page and quickly find the information they are looking for. Headings make content more accessible: For users with visual impairments who use screen readers, headings provide a way to navigate the content easily. This is because screen readers can read out the headings, allowing users to navigate to the relevant section quickly.

Headings help with SEO: Search engines use headings to understand the structure and content of a page. By using relevant and descriptive headings, you can help search engines to better understand the content of your page and improve your search engine rankings.

Importance of Maintaining Hierarchy:

1. Semantic Structure:
   Heading tags (`<h1>` to `<h6>`) provide semantic meaning to different sections of your content. They convey the hierarchy and relationships between different pieces of information.

2. Accessibility:
Screen readers and other assistive technologies use heading tags to navigate and understand the structure of a webpage. A well-organized heading hierarchy enhances accessibility for users with disabilities.

3. SEO (Search Engine Optimization):
   Search engines consider heading tags to understand the content structure and relevance.
   Properly structured headings contribute to better SEO, improving the visibility of your content in search engine results.

1. Main Heading (`<h1>`):
   - Role: Represents the main topic or section of the content.
   - Usage: Should be unique on a page, reflecting the overarching theme.

2. Paragraph (`<p>`):
   - Role: Contains the main text content.
   - Usage: Follows the main heading, providing detailed information.

3. Subheading (`<h2>`):
   - Role: Represents a subsection or subtopic related to the main heading.
   - Usage: Enhances the hierarchy, indicating a level below the main heading.

4. Another Paragraph (`<p>`):
   - Role: Contains additional text relevant to the subheading.
   - Usage: Supports the subheading, offering more detailed information.

Best Practices:
1. Sequential Order:
   - Always use heading tags in sequential order (`<h1>` to `<h6>`).

- Avoid skipping heading levels for a consistent and logical hierarchy.

2. Descriptive Headings:
- Ensure each heading provides a clear and concise description of the content it precedes.

3. Avoid Styling for Size: - Use CSS to style headings for visual presentation, but avoid using larger sizes solely for styling purposes.

4. Limit Usage:
- Use headings to represent meaningful sections, avoiding overuse for stylistic purposes.

Example with CSS Styling:

```
<style>
 h1 {
  color: #333;
  font-size: 24px;
  /* Additional styling as needed */
 }
 h2 {
  color: #666;
  font-size: 20px;
  /* Additional styling as needed */
 }
 p {
  color: #999;
  font-size: 16px;
  /* Additional styling as needed */
 }
 </style>
<h1>Main Heading</h1>
<p>Paragraph of text.</p>
<h2>Subheading</h2>
<p>Another paragraph of text.</p>
```

In this example, CSS is used for visual styling while maintaining the semantic structure provided by the HTML heading tags. This ensures a harmonious blend of content hierarchy and visual presentation.

CSS or Cascading Style Sheets is a powerful tool that is used to stylize and add aesthetic appeal to web pages. It can be used to separate the content and presentation of a website, making it easier to maintain and update.

This approach ensures that the hierarchy of the content is maintained, while also providing visual appeal.

Enhance Accessibility with Alt Attributes:

When including images, always add descriptive `alt` attributes to enhance accessibility for users with visual impairments.

```
<img src="image.jpg" alt="A descriptive text about the image">
```

Alt attributes are an essential part of website accessibility, as they provide context for users who cannot see images due to visual impairments. Here are some tips for using alt attributes effectively: Be descriptive: Your alt text should provide a clear and accurate description of the image. Use specific details and avoid vague language or generic phrases like "image" or "picture".

Keep it concise: Alt text should be brief and to the point. Aim for 125 characters or less, and avoid unnecessary details or irrelevant information.

Consider context: Alt text should reflect the purpose of the image and the surrounding content. For example, if the image is a chart or graph, the alt text should summarize the data it presents.

Don't duplicate content: If the image already has a caption or title, don't repeat the same information in the alt text. Instead, provide additional context or details that are not included in the caption. Test for effectiveness: Use accessibility tools and screen readers to test your alt text and ensure that it provides a meaningful description of the image.

By following these guidelines, you can ensure that your website is accessible to all users, regardless of their visual abilities. Remember, accessibility is not just a legal requirement, it's also a moral and ethical responsibility to create an inclusive online community.

Tips for Writing Clean HTML Code:

Use Semantic HTML:
Semantics refer to the meaning of a piece of code. Use semantic HTML to give your code more meaning and make it easier to read. For instance, use `header` and `footer` tags to mark the beginning and end of a web page. Use `nav` tag for navigational links and `article` tag for main content.

Use Consistent Naming Conventions:
Use a consistent naming convention for your HTML elements. This makes it easier to read and understand your code. For instance, use lowercase and hyphens to separate words in an element's name. Avoid using spaces or underscores.
*Use Alt Text for Images:**
Add alt text to your images. This is important for accessibility purposes, as screen readers can read out the alt text to visually impaired users. Additionally, if an image fails to load, the alt text will be displayed instead, providing context to the user.

Avoid Inline Styles:
Inline styles can make your HTML code harder to read and maintain. Instead, use external CSS files or add styles to the head section of your HTML document. This makes it easier to manage and update the styling of your web pages.

Validate Your Code:
Validate your HTML code to ensure that it is error-free and adheres to the latest web standards.

This can be done using online tools such as the W3C Markup Validation Service. Validating your code helps to prevent issues such as broken links, missing tags, and other errors that can negatively impact your website's performance and user experience.

Indentation and Formatting:

Keep your code well-indented and organized. This improves readability and makes it easier for you and other developers to understand the structure.

```
<div>
    <p>Indented content for clarity.</p>
</div>
```

Avoid Unnecessary Divs:

Minimize the use of generic `<div>` elements for styling purposes. Instead, rely on semantic tags and CSS classes to style your content.

```
<article class="styled-article">    <!-- Content goes here -->   </article>
```

Use the appropriate HTML tag for each content type, such as `<h1>` for main headings, `<p>` for paragraphs, `<ul>` for unordered lists, and `<ol>` for ordered lists.

Avoid using tables for layout purposes, as they are primarily intended for displaying tabular data. Instead, use CSS layout techniques such as flexbox or grid.

Use the `alt` attribute for images to provide a text description that can be read by screen readers and search engines. Use the `title` attribute for links to provide additional context or information about the linked page. Avoid using inline styles, as they can make your code harder to maintain and override. Instead, use CSS classes to apply styles consistently across your website.

Use indentation and comments to make your code more readable and easier to understand for other developers.

By following these practices, you can create HTML that is easy to read, maintain, and understand for both developers and users. Remember, writing clean and semantic HTML is not only good for accessibility and SEO, but it also contributes to a better user experience overall. Adhering to semantic HTML best practices not only makes your code more readable but also contributes to better accessibility and improved search engine optimization. By choosing meaningful tags and following clean coding conventions, you enhance both the developer experience and the overall usability of your web pages.

The Power of Header Element:

"Dive deep into the Header element, your website's first impression. Uncover its role in providing structure and meaning to your content. Learn how to utilize <header> to create visually appealing and functionally rich introductory sections on your web pages."

The <header> element is an HTML5 semantic element that represents introductory content, typically a group of introductory or navigational aids.

The <header> element can define a global site header, described as a banner in the accessibility tree. It usually includes a logo, company name, search feature, and possibly the global navigation or a slogan

Here's an example of how you might use the <header> element to create visually appealing and functionally rich introductory sections on your web pages:

```
<header>
  <img src="logo.png" alt="Logo">
  <nav>
   <ul>
    <li><a href="#">Home</a></li>
    <li><a href="#">About</a></li>
    <li><a href="#">Contact</a></li>
   </ul>
  </nav>
  <h1>Welcome to My Website</h1>
  <p>Here you will find all the information you need about our products and services.</p>
  <form action="#" method="get">
   <input type="text" name="search" placeholder="Search...">
   <button type="submit">Go</button>
  </form>
</header>
```

In this example, we've used the <header> element to create an introductory section for a website. We've included a logo, navigation menu, heading, paragraph, and search form.

The <header> element is a powerful tool that can help create a visually appealing and functional introductory section for your website. Here are some additional tips and tricks for using the <header> element effectively:

Consider the purpose and audience of your website when designing your header. For example, a corporate website may want to include a company logo and tagline, whereas a personal blog may want to focus on the author's name and photo. Use semantic HTML to make your header more accessible to users with disabilities. For example, include alt text for images and use headings to provide structure and hierarchy.

Keep your header concise and organized. Include only the most important elements and use subheadings or other design elements to separate different sections.
Use CSS to style your header and make it stand out. This can include font choices, color schemes, and background images. Consider using JavaScript or other interactive elements to make your header more dynamic. For example, you could use a dropdown menu for navigation or include a slideshow of images.

Overall, the <header> element is a versatile and powerful tool that can help create an engaging and informative introductory section for your website. By following these tips and experimenting with different design elements, you can create a header that is both visually appealing and functionally rich.

Navigating with Nav Element:

"Unlock the potential of the Nav element, your site's navigation maestro. Discover how to organize and present navigation links effectively, enhancing both user experience and search engine visibility. Turn your <nav> into a user-friendly guide for seamless website exploration."

The <nav> element is an HTML5 semantic element that represents a section of a page whose purpose is to provide navigation links, either within the current document or to other documents.

The <nav> element is intended only for a major block of navigation links. It is not necessary for all links to be contained in a <nav> element.

Here's an example of how you might use the <nav> element to organize and present navigation links effectively:

```
<nav>
  <ul>
   <li><a href="#">Home</a></li>
   <li><a href="#">About Us</a></li>
   <li><a href="#">Products</a></li>
   <li><a href="#">Services</a></li>
   <li><a href="#">Contact Us</a></li>
  </ul>
</nav>
```

In this example, we've used the <nav> element to create a navigation menu with a list of links. The <ul> element contains an unordered list of links, and each link is represented by an <a> element.

The <nav> element is a crucial component of website design. Here are some best practices to keep in mind when using the <nav> element:

Keep the navigation menu simple: A navigation menu should be easy to understand and use. Try to keep the number of links to a minimum and organize them in a logical manner.

Use clear and concise labels: The labels for the links should be clear and concise, using simple language that the user will easily understand.

Use a consistent layout: A consistent layout will help users navigate your site more easily. Use the same layout and style for all pages on your site.

Make the navigation menu visible: The navigation menu should be clearly visible and easy to find. Generally, it is located at the top of the page or in the sidebar.

Use dropdown menus where appropriate: If you have a large number of links, you can use dropdown menus to organize them. This will make it easier for users to find what they are looking for.

Use descriptive link text: The link text should be descriptive and explain exactly what the user can expect to find when they click the link.

Test your navigation menu: Finally, it's important to test your navigation menu to make sure it works properly. Make sure all links are working and that the menu is easy to use on both desktop and mobile devices.

By following these best practices, you can create a user-friendly navigation menu that will enhance the user experience on your website. Remember, the primary goal of the navigation menu is to help users find what they are looking for quickly and easily.

Crafting Compelling Articles:

"Master the Article element to create engaging and standalone content pieces. Whether you're a blogger, journalist, or content creator, <article> is your key to structuring and presenting information in a way that captivates both readers and search engines."

The <article> element is an HTML5 semantic element that represents a self-contained piece of content, such as a blog post or news article.

Using the <article> element can help improve the accessibility and search engine optimization (SEO) of your website. Screen readers for disabled users can use this element to determine whether to omit the initial rendering of this content.

Here's an example of how you might use the <article> element to create engaging and standalone content pieces:

```
<article>
  <h2>Article Title</h2>
  <p>Article content goes here...</p>
</article>
```

In this example, we've used the <article> element to create a self-contained piece of content with a heading and paragraph.

Choose a captivating headline: The title of your article should be attention-grabbing and accurately reflect the content of the article. Use clear and concise language and try to include relevant keywords that people might use when searching for information on the topic.

Use subheadings: Break up your article into sections using subheadings. This makes it easier for readers to scan through and find the information they need. It also helps with SEO, as search engines can use these headings to understand the structure of your article.

Keep paragraphs short: Long paragraphs can be overwhelming and difficult to read. Aim to keep your paragraphs to no more than three or four sentences. This makes your content more digestible and easier to follow.

Incorporate multimedia: Including images, videos, and other multimedia can help break up the text and make your article more engaging. Just make sure that any multimedia you use is relevant to the content of your article.

Provide value: Your article should provide value to your readers. Whether it's offering helpful tips, sharing your expertise, or providing insights on a particular topic, make sure that your content is informative and useful.

By following these tips and using the <article> element effectively, you can create compelling and engaging articles that will captivate both readers and search engines.

Sectioning for Success:

"Explore the versatility of the Section element. Learn how to organize your content logically using <section>, providing clarity and structure to your web pages. This chapter is your guide to creating a well-organized and easily maintainable website."

The <section> element is an HTML5 semantic element that represents a standalone section of content on a web page. It is used to group related content together and provide structure and clarity to the page.

Using the <section> element can help improve the accessibility and search engine optimization (SEO) of your website. Screen readers for disabled users can use this element to determine whether to omit the initial rendering of this content.

Here's an example of how you might use the <section> element to create a well-organized and easily maintainable website:

```
<section>
  <h2>Section Title</h2>
  <p>Section content goes here...</p>
</section>
```

In this example, we've used the <section> element to create a standalone section of content with a heading and paragraph.

By using the <section> element, you can organize your content logically and make it easier for users to navigate your website. This can help improve the user experience and make your website more appealing to visitors.

Building a Solid Foundation with Footer:
"Conclude your web pages with a strong foundation using the Footer element. From copyright information to contact details, <footer> is where your site leaves a lasting impression. Discover how to use this element to enhance professionalism and user engagement."

The <footer> element is an HTML5 semantic element that represents a footer section for a document or a section.

Using the <footer> element can help improve the accessibility and search engine optimization (SEO) of your website. Screen readers for disabled users can use this element to determine whether to omit the initial rendering of this content.

Here's an example of how you might use the <footer> element to enhance professionalism and user engagement:

```
<footer>
  <p>&copy; My Website 2023</p>
  <p>Contact us at info@mywebsite.com</p>
  <ul>
   <li><a href="#">Privacy Policy</a></li>
   <li><a href="#">Terms of Use</a></li>
   <li><a href="#">Site Map</a></li>
  </ul>
</footer>
```

In this example, we've used the <footer> element to create a footer section with copyright information, contact details, and links to other pages.

Real-world Applications:
"Put your knowledge to the test with real-world examples. This chapter provides hands-on exercises and projects, allowing you to apply your understanding of Semantic HTML elements in practical scenarios. Get ready to take your skills to the next level."

The real-world applications of Semantic HTML elements are vast and varied. By using semantic elements, you can create web pages that are more accessible, more search engine friendly, and easier to maintain.

Here are some examples of how you might use Semantic HTML elements in practical scenarios:

1. Blog Posts: Use the <article> element to create standalone pieces of content, such as blog posts or news articles.
2. Navigation Menus: Use the <nav> element to create navigation menus that are easy to navigate and understand.
3. Header: The <header> element is used to define a header section for a document or a section. It usually contains a logo, navigation menu, and other introductory content.
4. Nav: The <nav> element is used to define a section of navigation links.
5. Article: The <article> element is used to define an independent, self-contained piece of content, such as a blog post or news article.
6. Section: The <section> element is used to define a section of related content.
7. Footers: The <footer> element is used to define a footer section for a document or a section. It usually contains copyright information, contact details, links to other pages and other closing content.
8. Product Listings: Use the <section> element to group related content together, such as product listings or news stories.
9. Forms: Use the <form> element to create forms that are easy to fill out and submit.

By using Semantic HTML elements in your web pages, you can create a more professional and user-friendly experience for your visitors. By using these semantic elements, you can create web pages that are more accessible, more search engine friendly, and easier to maintain. For example, screen readers for disabled users can use these elements to determine whether to omit the initial rendering of this content. Search engines can also use these elements to identify the primary content areas in the document.

How Semantic HTML Benefits SEO
Semantic HTML refers to syntax that makes the HTML more comprehensible by better defining the different sections and layout of web pages.
Using Semantic HTML can help improve the accessibility and search engine optimization (SEO) of your website. Screen readers for disabled users can use these elements to determine whether to omit the initial rendering of this content.

By using Semantic HTML elements in your web pages, you can create a more professional and user-friendly experience for your visitors. This can help improve the user experience and make your website more appealing to visitors.
Semantic HTML elements provide a clear structure and meaning to your website, making it easier for search engines to understand and index your content.
Here's an example of how you might use Semantic HTML elements to improve the SEO of your

website:

```
<header>
 <h1>My Website</h1>
 <nav>
  <ul>
   <li><a href="#">Home</a></li>
   <li><a href="#">About</a></li>
   <li><a href="#">Contact</a></li>
  </ul>
 </nav>
</header>
<main>
 <article>
  <h2>Article Title</h2>
  <p>Article content goes here...</p>
 </article>
 <section>
  <h2>Section Title</h2>
  <p>Section content goes here...</p>
 </section>
 <aside>
  <h2>Aside Title</h2>
  <p>Aside content goes here...</p>
 </aside>
</main>
<footer>
 <p>&copy; My Website 2023</p>
 <p>Contact us at info@mywebsite.com</p>
</footer>
```

In this example, we've used Semantic HTML elements to create a well-structured web page with a header, main content area, and footer. The <header> element contains a logo and navigation menu, while the <main> element contains articles, sections, and asides. The <footer> element contains copyright information and contact details.

By using Semantic HTML elements in your web pages, you can create a more professional and user-friendly experience for your visitors. This can help improve the user experience and make your website more appealing to visitors.

HTML TABLES

Creating Tables

HTML tables are used to display data in a tabular format. To create a table, you can use the <table> element. Inside the <table> element, you can use the <tr> element to define a row, and the <td> element to define a cell. HTML tables are essential for organizing and presenting data in a structured format. In this section, we will explore the process of creating tables using HTML tags.

Here's an example of how to create a simple table:

Basic Table Structure:

To create a basic table, use the `<table>`, `<tr>` (table row), `<th>` (table header), and `<td>` (table data) tags.

```
<table>
 <tr>
  <th>Header 1</th>
  <th>Header 2</th>
 </tr>
 <tr>
  <td>Row 1, Cell 1</td>
  <td>Row 1, Cell 2</td>
 </tr>
 <tr>
  <td>Row 2, Cell 1</td>
  <td>Row 2, Cell 2</td>
 </tr>
</table>
```

Spanning Rows and Columns:

Use the `colspan` and `rowspan` attributes to make a cell span multiple columns or rows.

```
<table>
 <tr>
  <th colspan="2">Header 1 and 2</th>
 </tr>
 <tr>
  <td rowspan="2">Row 1, Cell 1</td>
```

```
    <td>Row 1, Cell 2</td>
  </tr>
  <tr>
    <td>Row 2, Cell 2</td>
  </tr>
</table>
```

Formatting Tables:

You can also format tables using CSS. Formatting is crucial to ensure tables are visually appealing and easy to understand. Let's explore various formatting techniques.

For example, you can use the border property to add borders to your table cells:

```
table {
  border-collapse: collapse;
}
td {
  border: 1px solid black;
}
```

This CSS code will collapse the borders of the table cells and add a black border around each cell. Adding Borders and Styling:

Use CSS to add borders and style to your tables. You can apply styles to the table, headers, and cells.

```
<style>
  table {
    border-collapse: collapse;
    width: 100%;
  }
  th, td {
    border: 1px solid #dddddd;
    text-align: left;
    padding: 8px;   }
</style>
```

2. Alternating Row Colors:
   Improve readability by applying alternating colors to rows.

```
tr:nth-child(even) {
  background-color: #f2f2f2;}
```

Making Tables Accessible

To make tables accessible, you should use the <th> element to define header cells and the <caption> element to provide a summary of the table contents. You should also use the scope attribute to associate header cells with their corresponding data cells. Creating accessible tables is essential for users with disabilities. Let's discuss practices for making tables accessible.

Using `<caption>` for Table Description:
   Include a `<caption>` tag to provide a brief description of the table's content.

```
<table>
<caption>
 Monthly Sales Report
</caption>
<tr>
 <th scope="col">Product</th>
 <th scope="col">Sales</th>
</tr>
<tr>
 <td>Product A</td>
 <td>1000</td>
</tr>
<tr>
 <td>Product B</td>
 <td>750</td>
</tr>
</table>
```

In this case, the <caption> provides a brief description of the table's purpose, and the scope attribute is used to indicate that the header cells pertain to columns. These practices enhance the accessibility of the table for users with diverse needs.

By understanding the creation, formatting, and accessibility considerations of HTML tables, you can design tables that not only convey data effectively but also provide a positive user experience for all visitors to your website.

Using `<th>` for Header Cells:
The `<th>` element is used to define header cells in a table. These cells should contain the titles or labels for the data in the corresponding column or row. The `scope` attribute can be used to specify whether the header cell pertains to a row or column. It is important to ensure that header cells are associated with their corresponding data cells using the `id` and `headers` attributes.

Using `aria-label` for Table Description:
In addition to using the `<caption>` element, you can also use the `aria-label` attribute to provide a description of the table contents. This attribute can be added to the `<table>` element and should contain a brief description of the table's purpose.

Providing Descriptive Headers in HTML Tables:
HTML tables often include header cells to label the content in each column or row. To enhance the semantic structure of tables and make them more accessible, the <th> (table header) element is utilized. The scope attribute is employed to associate header cells with either columns (col) or rows (row).

Use `<th>` with the `scope` attribute to associate headers with rows or columns. The concept of providing descriptive headers using <th> with the scope attribute.

Example:
Consider a table representing monthly revenue:

```
<table>
 <tr>
  <th scope="col">Month</th>
  <th scope="col">Revenue</th>
 </tr>
 <tr>
  <td>January</td>
  <td>$10,000</td>
 </tr>
 <tr>
  <td>February</td>
  <td>$12,500</td>
 </tr>
 <!-- More data rows go here -->
</table>
```

In this example, <th> elements are used for the header cells, indicating that they pertain to columns. The scope="col" attribute explicitly states that the headers apply to columns. This not only provides a clear structure but also assists screen readers in interpreting the content correctly.

Always use the <th> element to define header cells in a table. This helps to distinguish them from regular cells and provides context for screen readers. Use the scope attribute to define whether the header cell applies to a column or a row. This is particularly important for screen reader users who may be navigating through the table using a keyboard.

Avoid using merged cells in tables, as they can make it difficult for screen readers to interpret the table's structure. If you do need to merge cells, make sure to use the headers attribute to provide additional context. If your table has a lot of data, consider using the caption element to provide an overall description of the table's purpose. This can be particularly helpful for users who are visually impaired and may not be able to see the entire table at once.

Accessibility Considerations:

Screen Readers:
Screen readers rely on semantic HTML to convey information to users with visual impairments. Using <th> with the appropriate scope attribute helps screen readers announce header information accurately.

Table Navigation:
Assistive technologies often provide users with the ability to navigate tables by row or column headers.
Associating headers correctly enhances the navigational experience for users with disabilities.

Screen readers are assistive technologies that help users with visual impairments to access digital content. They rely on semantic HTML to convey information to users. Semantic HTML is a way of writing HTML that emphasizes the meaning of the content rather than its presentation. Semantic HTML uses specific tags to describe the content of a web page, making it easier for screen readers and other assistive technologies to understand the structure of the page [1].

To make tables accessible, you should use the `<th>` element to define header cells and the `scope` attribute to associate header cells with their corresponding data cells. This helps screen readers announce header information accurately. You should also use the `summary` attribute to provide a summary of the table contents, and the `caption` element to provide a caption for the table [2].

Assistive technologies often provide users with the ability to navigate tables by row or column headers. Associating headers correctly enhances the navigational experience for users with disabilities. You can use the `headers` attribute to associate data cells with their corresponding header cells [2].

To create an accessible table, you can use the following techniques:
- Use the `<caption>` element to provide a caption for the table.
- Use the `<thead>` element to define the table header.
- Use the `<tbody>` element to define the table body.
- Use the `<tr>` element to define table rows.
- Use the `<th>` element with the `scope` attribute to define header cells.
- Use the `headers` attribute to associate data cells with their corresponding header cells.

Here's an example of how you might use these techniques to create an accessible table:

```html
<table>
 <caption>Monthly Sales Report</caption>
 <thead>
  <tr>
   <th scope="col">Month</th>
   <th scope="col">Sales</th>
  </tr>
 </thead>
 <tbody>
  <tr>
   <th scope="row">January</th>
   <td>$1000</td>
  </tr>
  <tr>
   <th scope="row">February</th>
   <td>$1500</td>
  </tr>
 </tbody>
</table>
```

In this example, we've used the `<th>` element with the `scope` attribute to define header cells, and the `headers` attribute to associate data cells with their corresponding header cells.

Best Practices:
Always use <th> for header cells rather than regular <td> cells.
Specify the scope attribute to indicate whether the header pertains to a column (col) or a row (row).

Provide meaningful and descriptive header content to enhance understanding.
By incorporating these practices, you contribute to creating accessible and well-structured tables that cater to a diverse audience.

By mastering the creation and formatting of HTML tables and ensuring accessibility, you can effectively present data in a structured and visually appealing manner. These skills are fundamental for building user-friendly and inclusive web pages.

HTML FORMS: ADVANCED

Form Validation:

Form validation is a crucial aspect of web development that ensures the data submitted through forms is accurate and meets specified criteria. This chapter explores advanced techniques for validating user input within

HTML forms.

Client-Side Validation:

- Utilize JavaScript to perform validation on the client side before the form is submitted.
- Examples of client-side validation include checking for required fields, email formats, and password strength.

```html
<form onsubmit="return validateForm()">
  <!-- Form fields go here -->
  <input type="submit" value="Submit">
</form>
<script>
  function validateForm() {
    // Validation logic goes here
    if (/* Validation fails */) {
      alert("Please fill out all required fields.");
      return false;
    }
    return true;
  }
</script>
```

Server-Side Validation:

- While client-side validation enhances user experience, server-side validation is essential for security.
- Validate input on the server to prevent malicious attempts to bypass client-side checks.

```php
<?php
// Server-side validation logic
if ($_SERVER["REQUEST_METHOD"] == "POST") {
  $username = validateInput($_POST["username"]);
  // Validate other fields
}
function validateInput($data) {
```

```
    // Validation logic goes here
}
?>
```

Validation Libraries:

While it is possible to write custom validation code for each form, it can be time-consuming and error-prone. Fortunately, there are many validation libraries available that can simplify this process. Some popular validation libraries include jQuery Validation, Laravel Validation, and Symfony Validator. These libraries provide pre-built validation rules for common validation scenarios, such as checking for required fields, email formats, and password strength. Using a validation library can save time and reduce the risk of errors in your validation code.

Form validation is an essential aspect of web development that ensures the accuracy and integrity of user-submitted data. While client-side validation is useful for enhancing user experience, it is essential to perform server-side validation as well to prevent malicious attacks and ensure data integrity. Utilizing a validation library can simplify the validation process and reduce the risk of errors.

Dropdowns, Text Areas, and Other Form Elements:

Beyond standard input fields, HTML provides various form elements for diverse user interactions. This chapter delves into the usage and customization of dropdowns, text areas, and other advanced form elements.

Dropdown Menus:

- Create dropdown menus with the `<select>` and `<option>` elements.
- Utilize the `multiple` attribute for multi-select dropdowns.

```
<select>
    <option value="option1">Option 1</option>
    <option value="option2">Option 2</option>
    <option value="option3">Option 3</option>
</select>
```

Dropdown menus are an essential part of web development as they allow users to select from a list of options.

To create a dropdown menu, use the `<select>` and `<option>` elements. The `<select>` element defines the dropdown menu, while the `<option>` element defines the options within the dropdown.
Use the `value` attribute to define the value associated with each option. This value will be sent to the server when the form is submitted.

To allow users to select multiple options, add the `multiple` attribute to the `<select>` element.
You can customize the appearance of your dropdown menu using CSS. Some popular CSS properties to use include `background-color`, `border`, `padding`, and `font-size`.

You can also use JavaScript to enhance the functionality of your dropdown menu. For example, you can use JavaScript to dynamically populate the options based on user input or to show and hide dropdowns based on user selections.

Text Areas:
Implement large text input areas with the `<textarea>` element.
Specify the number of rows and columns for the text area.
To create a text area, use the `<textarea>` element. The `rows` and `cols` attributes can be used to define the size of the text area.

Use the `placeholder` attribute to provide users with a hint of what to type in the text area.
You can customize the appearance of your text area using CSS. Some popular CSS properties to use include `background color`, `border`, `padding`, and `font-size`.

You can also use JavaScript to enhance the functionality of your text area. For example, you can use JavaScript to limit the number of characters that can be entered or to validate the input before submitting the form.

```
<textarea rows="4" cols="50">
  Enter your text here...
</textarea>
```

Use the `<textarea>` element to create a text area.

Specify the number of rows and columns using the `rows` and `cols` attributes. This will ensure that the text area is appropriately sized for the user's input. Consider using CSS to style your text area. You can adjust the font, background color, and border to create a more visually appealing input field.
Use JavaScript to validate user input. You can check for the length of the input and ensure that it meets any necessary criteria before submitting it to the server.

Consider using a JavaScript library to enhance the functionality of your text area. Libraries like TinyMCE and CKEditor provide additional features like spell checking, formatting options, and image uploading.

By following these tips, you can create a user-friendly text input area that meets the needs of your web application. Remember to test your text area thoroughly to ensure that it works as intended and provides a positive user experience.

Other Form Elements:
  - Explore advanced form elements like checkboxes, radio buttons, and file upload inputs.
  - Use the `<input>` element with different types and attributes to create varied form controls.

Checkboxes: Checkboxes allow users to select one or more options from a list. They are useful when you have a list of options and the user can select multiple options. You can create checkboxes using the `<input>` element with the `type="checkbox"` attribute.

Radio buttons: Radio buttons are similar to checkboxes, but they allow the user to select only one option from a list. You can create radio buttons using the `<input>` element with the `type="radio"` attribute. To group radio buttons, use the `name` attribute with the same value for each button in the group.

File upload inputs: File upload inputs allow users to upload files from their device. You can create a file upload input using the `<input>` element with the `type="file"` attribute. When the user selects a file to upload, the file's data is sent with the form submission.

In addition to these form elements, you can also use the following attributes with the `<input>` element to create more customized form controls:

placeholder: This attribute specifies a short hint that describes the expected value of an input field. It is displayed in the field until the user enters a value.

required: This attribute specifies that an input field must be filled out before submitting the form. If the user tries to submit the form without filling out a required field, an error message is displayed.

disabled: This attribute specifies that an input field should be disabled. A disabled field cannot be edited or submitted with the form.

By using these form elements and attributes, you can create more advanced and user-friendly forms that will help you collect the information you need from your users.

```html
<input type="checkbox" name="subscribe" value="yes"> Subscribe<br>
<input type="radio" name="gender" value="male"> Male
<input type="radio" name="gender" value="female"> Female<br>
<input type="file" name="fileToUpload" id="fileToUpload">
<!DOCTYPE html>
<html lang="en">
 <head>
  <meta charset="UTF-8" />
  <meta name="viewport" content="width=device-width, initial-scale=1.0" />
  <title>Form Elements</title>
  <style>
   table {
    width: 100%;
    border-collapse: collapse;
    margin-top: 20px;
   }
   th,
   td {
    border: 1px solid #ddd;
    padding: 8px;
    text-align: left;
   }
   th {
    background-color: #f2f2f2;
   }
  </style>
 </head>
 <body>
  <h2>Form Elements</h2>
```

```
<table>
 <thead>
  <tr>
   <th>Form Element</th>
   <th>Syntax</th>
   <th>Description</th>
  </tr>
 </thead>
 <tbody>
  <tr>
   <td><strong>Text Input</strong></td>
   <td><code>&lt;input type="text" name="username" /&gt;</code></td>
   <td>Single-line text input field for user input.</td>
  </tr>
  <tr>
   <td><strong>Password Input</strong></td>
   <td><code>&lt;input type="password" name="password" /&gt;</code></td>
   <td>Secure input for passwords, characters are usually masked.</td>
  </tr>
  <tr>
   <td><strong>Textarea</strong></td>
   <td><code>&lt;textarea name="message"&gt;&lt;/textarea&gt;</code></td>
   <td>Multi-line text input for longer messages or comments.</td>
  </tr>
  <tr>
   <td><strong>Radio Buttons</strong></td>
   <td>
    <code>&lt;input type="radio" name="gender" value="male" /&gt;</code>
   </td>
   <td>Allows users to select one option from a set of options.</td>
  </tr>
  <tr>
   <td><strong>Checkbox</strong></td>
   <td><code>&lt;input type="checkbox" name="subscribe" /&gt;</code></td>
   <td>Enables users to select multiple options or agree to terms.</td>
  </tr>
  <tr>
   <td><strong>Select Dropdown</strong></td>
   <td>
    <code>
     &lt;select name="country"&gt;<br />
       &lt;option value="usa"&gt;United
```

```
    States&lt;/option&gt;<br />
      &lt;option value="canada"&gt;Canada&lt;/option&gt;<br />
    &lt;/select&gt;
  </code>
 </td>
 <td>Dropdown menu for selecting a single option from a list.</td>
 </tr>
 <tr>
 <td><strong>Submit Button</strong></td>
 <td><code>&lt;input type="submit" value="Submit" /&gt;</code></td>
 <td>Submits the form data to the server for processing.</td>
 </tr>
 <tr>
 <td><strong>Reset Button</strong></td>
 <td><code>&lt;input type="reset" value="Reset" /&gt;</code></td>
 <td>Resets the form fields to their default values.</td>
 </tr>
 <tr>
 <td><strong>File Input</strong></td>
 <td><code>&lt;input type="file" name="file" /&gt;</code></td>
 <td>Allows users to upload files to the server.</td>
 </tr>
 </tbody>
 </table>
</body>
</html>
```

HTML Events:

This table provides a concise reference for various HTML events, their descriptions, and syntax. HTML events are actions or occurrences that happen on a web page. They can be initiated by the user, the browser, or the web page itself. Events can be added to HTML elements using the `on` attribute. For example, if you wanted to add a click event to a button, you would use the following code:

```
<button onclick="myFunction()">Click me!</button>
```

Here are some of the most commonly used HTML events:

HTML Event

Descriptions & Uses

Full Syntax with Accessibility

onclick

Triggered when a user clicks an element. Commonly used for handling button clicks or other interactive elements.

```
<button onclick="handlerFunction()" tabindex="0" role="button">Click me</button>
```

ondblclick

Fired when a user double-clicks an element. Useful for actions requiring a double-click gesture.

```
<button ondblclick="handlerFunction()" tabindex="0" role="button">
```

onmouseover

Occurs when the mouse pointer is moved over an element. Can be used for displaying additional information or effects.

```
<button onmouseover="handlerFunction()" aria-describedby="additionalInfo">
```

onmouseout

Triggered when the mouse pointer leaves an element. Useful for reverting changes made by onmouseover.

```
<button onmouseout="handlerFunction()">
```

onmousedown

Fired when the mouse button is pressed on an element. Often used to initiate an action on click and hold.

```
<button onmousedown="handlerFunction()" role="button">
```

onmouseup

Occurs when the mouse button is released after being pressed. Can be used in combination with onmousedown.

```
<button onmouseup="handlerFunction()" role="button">
```

onchange

Typically used with form elements like <input> or <select>. Triggered when the value of the element is changed.

```
<input type="text" onchange="handlerFunction()">
```

onsubmit

Used in <form> elements to handle form submission. Executed when the form is submitted either through a button or enter key.

```
<form onsubmit="handlerFunction()">
```

onfocus

Fired when an element receives focus, usually via tab navigation or click. Useful for providing feedback or additional information.

```
<input type="text" onfocus="handlerFunction()">
```

onblur

Occurs when an element loses focus. Helpful for validating input or triggering actions when a user leaves a field.

```
<input type="text" onblur="handlerFunction()">
```

onkeydown

Triggered when a key is pressed down. Useful for handling keyboard input, such as shortcuts or navigation.

```
<input type="text" onkeydown="handlerFunction()">
```

onkeyup

Fired when a key is released after being pressed. Can be used for real-time validation or other dynamic interactions.

```
<input type="text" onkeyup="handlerFunction()">
```

onkeypress

Similar to onkeydown, but specifically for printable characters.

```
<input type="text" onkeypress="handlerFunction()">
```

onload

Invoked when a page or an element finishes loading. Often used to initialize scripts or perform setup tasks.

```
<body onload="handlerFunction()">
```

ontouchstart

Triggered when a touch point is placed on the touch surface. Used in mobile and touch-enabled interfaces.

```
<button ontouchstart="handlerFunction()" role="button">
```

ontouchend

> Fired when a touch point is removed from the touch surface.

> `<button ontouchend="handlerFunction()" role="button">`

ontouchmove

> Occurs when a touch point is moved along the touch surface. Useful for tracking touch gestures or interactions.

> `<slider ontouchmove="handlerFunction()" role="slider">`

ontouchcancel

> Triggered when a touch event is interrupted or canceled. Commonly used to clean up resources associated with touch events.

> `<button ontouchcancel="handlerFunction()">`

Styling Forms:

Aesthetically pleasing forms enhance user experience. This chapter explores styling techniques to make forms visually appealing and in harmony with the overall design of a web page.

To create visually appealing forms, designers can use the following styling techniques:

Color: Choose colors that complement the overall design of the web page. Use a color scheme that is easy on the eyes and provides enough contrast between the background and foreground colors. Avoid using too many colors as it can make the form look cluttered.

Typography: Select a font that is easy to read and matches the tone of the website. Use font sizes that are appropriate for the content in the form. Use bold or italicized text to highlight important information.

Layout: Use a layout that is simple and easy to navigate. Group related fields together and use white space to separate different sections. Use labels and placeholders to indicate the purpose of each field. Buttons: Use buttons that are easy to click and blend in with the overall design of the form. Use colors and hover effects to make the buttons stand out.

Icons: Use icons to enhance the visual appeal of the form and to convey meaning quickly. Use icons that are relevant to the content in the form.

By applying these styling techniques, designers can create forms that are not only visually appealing but also enhance the user experience. A well-designed form can increase user engagement and make it easier for users to complete their tasks.

CSS Styling: - Apply CSS styles to form elements to control their appearance.
  - Utilize properties like `color`, `background`, and `border` to customize the look of input fields, buttons, and other form components.

CSS styling is an essential aspect of web development. Once you have created your HTML form, you can use CSS to customize the appearance of your form elements.

Here are some tips for applying CSS styles to your form components:
Use the `color` property to set the text color of your form elements. This can be useful for making your labels and input fields easier to read.

The `background` property allows you to set the background color of your form elements. You can use this to create a consistent look and feel across your form.

The `border` property lets you set the border style, width, and color of your form elements. You can use this to add some visual interest to your form or to make certain elements stand out.

Other properties you can use to customize your form include `padding`, `margin`, and `font-size`. These can be used to adjust the spacing and font size of your form elements.

When styling your form components, it's important to keep accessibility in mind. Make sure that your form is easy to navigate and that users can easily distinguish between different form elements.

In addition to using CSS, you can also use JavaScript to add interactivity to your form. For example, you can use JavaScript to validate user input or to display error messages when a user enters invalid data.

Example code:
```
input[type=text] {
    padding: 10px;
    border: 1px solid #ccc;
    border-radius: 4px;
}

button {
    background-color: #4CAF50;
    color: white;
    padding: 10px 15px;
    border: none;
    border-radius: 4px;
}
```

Responsive Design:
- Ensure forms are responsive and adapt well to different screen sizes.
- Use media queries to adjust styles based on the device's characteristics.

```
@media only screen and (max-width: 600px) {
    /* Styles for smaller screens */
    input[type=text] {
        width: 100%;
    }
}
```

Mastering advanced form techniques, including validation, diverse form elements, and stylish designs, contributes to creating dynamic and user-friendly web forms. These skills empower developers to build interactive and visually appealing interfaces that cater to diverse user interactions.

To further improve the responsiveness of web forms, there are additional techniques that developers can implement:

Use flexbox or grid layout to create more flexible and adaptive form layouts that can respond to different screen sizes and device orientations. Implement touch-friendly inputs, such as larger buttons and checkboxes, to make it easier for users to interact with forms on touch-enabled devices. Use HTML5 form validation to ensure that users enter valid data and provide helpful error messages when necessary. Consider using client-side form validation libraries, such as jQuery Validation or Parsley.js, to provide more advanced validation features and improve the user experience.

Experiment with different form designs and layouts to find the most effective and visually appealing options for your specific use case. Conduct user testing to gather feedback on your forms and identify areas for improvement. This can help you identify pain points and optimize your forms for better usability and user satisfaction. By implementing these techniques, developers can create web forms that are not only responsive and adaptable, but also highly functional and user-friendly.

HTML META TAGS FOR SEO

Introduction<a name="introduction"></a>
Meta tags are snippets of text that describe a page's content but don't appear on the page itself. They play a crucial role in SEO (Search Engine Optimization) by providing information to search engines and social media platforms about the content of your webpage. In this guide, we'll explore various HTML meta tags, focusing on those essential for SEO.

Title, Description, and Keywords

Title Tag:
The title tag is one of the most critical meta tags for SEO. It defines the title of your webpage, which appears as the main text in search engine results. A well-crafted title can significantly impact click-through rates.

The <title> element is used to define the title of a web page. It should be placed inside the <head> section of your HTML document.

Here's an example:
```
<head>
   <title>Your Page Title</title>
</head>
```

Meta Description Tag:
The meta description tag provides a brief summary of the page content. Although not a direct ranking factor, an engaging meta description can influence user clicks from search results. The <meta> element is used to define metadata about an HTML document. Here's an example:

```
<head>
   <meta name="description" content="Brief description of your page content">
</head>
```

Meta Keywords Tag:
In the past, search engines used the meta keywords tag to understand page content. However, major search engines now ignore it. Including a meta keywords tag is optional and may be omitted.

```
<head>
   <meta name="keywords" content="keyword1, keyword2, keyword3">
</head>
```

The keywords meta tag is no longer a significant factor in SEO. It was previously used to inform search engines about the keywords related to a webpage, but it was often abused by webmasters to manipulate search rankings. Nowadays, most search engines ignore this meta tag.

While it was once common practice to include a meta keywords tag in the head section of a webpage, major search engines like Google no longer use this tag as a ranking factor. This means that including a meta keywords tag is now optional and can be omitted altogether.

However, if you choose to include a meta keywords tag, it's important to do so correctly. Here are some best practices to follow:

Keep it short and sweet: Including too many keywords can actually hurt your search engine rankings, so it's best to limit your meta keywords tag to a few relevant keywords or phrases.

Use unique keywords: Avoid using the same keywords across multiple pages on your website. Instead, use unique keywords that accurately reflect the content of each individual page.

Don't stuff keywords: Keyword stuffing, or the practice of including the same keyword multiple times in a meta keywords tag, can actually hurt your search engine rankings. Instead, use a variety of relevant keywords that accurately reflect the content of your page.

Focus on quality content: While including a meta keywords tag can help search engines understand the content of your page, it's not a substitute for high-quality content. Make sure your webpage is well-written, informative, and engaging to attract and retain visitors.

Other Meta Tags :
There are several other meta tags that can be useful for SEO, including:
Robots meta tag: This tag instructs search engine crawlers about how to index your webpage. You can use it to prevent certain pages from being indexed, for example.

Canonical URL tag: This tag specifies the preferred URL for a web page when there are multiple versions of the same content available.

Open Graph tags and Twitter Cards:
These tags provide information to social media platforms about how to display your webpage when it's shared on their platforms. They can include information like the title, description, and image.

Using meta tags correctly can have a significant impact on your website's SEO. By providing accurate and relevant information to search engines and social media platforms, you can improve your website's visibility and attract more visitors. Remember to use the title, description, and other meta tags appropriately, and avoid keyword stuffing or other black hat SEO techniques.

Open Graph Protocol<a name="open-graph-protocol"></a>

The Open Graph Protocol enables your web pages to become rich objects in social media sharing. It controls how your content appears when shared on platforms like Facebook.

```
<head>
    <meta property="og:title" content="Your Open Graph Title">
    <meta property="og:description" content="Description of your content for social sharing">
    <meta property="og:image" content="URL to an image representing your content">
    <meta property="og:url" content="URL of the page">
```

```
</head>
```

Twitter Cards<a name="twitter-cards"></a>

Similar to Open Graph, Twitter Cards help control how your content is displayed when shared on Twitter. They enhance the appearance of your tweets.

```
<head>
    <meta name="twitter:card" content="summary">
    <meta name="twitter:title" content="Your Twitter Card Title">
    <meta name="twitter:description" content="Description of your content for Twitter">
    <meta name="twitter:image" content="URL to an image representing your content">
</head>
```

Best Practices:
<a name="best-practices"></a>

- Craft unique and compelling titles and descriptions for each page.
- Keep titles under 60 characters and meta descriptions under 155 characters.
- Use relevant keywords naturally in your content.
- Ensure Open Graph and Twitter Card images are of high quality.

<a name="conclusion"></a>

Optimizing HTML meta tags is a fundamental aspect of SEO. By implementing these best practices and leveraging Open Graph and Twitter Cards, you can enhance your website's visibility on search engines and improve its appearance on social media platforms. Stay updated with industry trends to adapt your meta tag strategy for continued SEO success.

Overall, while the meta keywords tag may no longer be a major ranking factor for search engines, it's still a good practice to include one for the sake of accuracy and organization. Just make sure to follow these best practices to ensure that your meta keywords tag is effective and doesn't harm your search engine rankings.

The Open Graph Protocol and Twitter Cards are essential tools for optimizing your website's social media sharing potential. By implementing Open Graph, your web pages can become rich objects on social media platforms like Facebook. The protocol enables you to control how your content appears when shared on these platforms. To implement Open Graph, you need to use HTML meta tags to define the title, description, image, and URL of your content.

Similarly, Twitter Cards also help control how your content is displayed when shared on Twitter. They are designed to enhance the appearance of your tweets and provide additional context to your followers. To implement Twitter Cards, you need to add HTML meta tags to your website's head section.
Both Open Graph and Twitter Cards are powerful tools for boosting your website's visibility and engagement on social media. By utilizing them effectively, you can increase your website's reach and drive more traffic to your site.

Here are some additional best practices to consider when optimizing your website for search engines:

Conduct keyword research to identify keywords and phrases that your target audience is searching for. Use these keywords in your content, but avoid overusing them. Aim for a keyword density of 1-2%.

Use header tags (H1, H2, H3, etc.) to structure your content. This makes it easier for search engines to understand the hierarchy of your information.

Use alt tags for images to describe what the image is about. This not only helps with accessibility, but also provides search engines with additional information about your content.

Make sure your website is mobile-friendly. With more and more people browsing the web on their mobile devices, having a responsive website is crucial for a good user experience.

Use internal linking to connect related content on your website. This helps search engines understand the structure of your website and can improve your website's ranking. Remember, while it's important to optimize your website for search engines, it's equally important to write for your audience. Create valuable, informative content that your target audience will find helpful and engaging.

In conclusion, by following these best practices, you can improve your website's ranking on search engines and attract more traffic to your site. Optimizing HTML meta tags is a fundamental aspect of SEO. By implementing these best practices and leveraging Open Graph and Twitter Cards, you can enhance your website's visibility on search engines and improve its appearance on social media platforms. Stay updated with industry trends to adapt your meta tag strategy for continued SEO success.

Meta tags play a crucial role in optimizing a website for search engines. Here are some tips to help you make the most out of your meta tags:

Title Tag: This is the most important meta tag as it appears in search engine results and is the first thing that users see when they come across your website. Make sure it accurately describes the content on your page and includes relevant keywords. Meta Description: This tag appears below the title tag in search engine results and provides a brief summary of the page's content. It should be between 50-160 characters long, include relevant keywords and entice users to click on the link. Open Graph Tags: These tags are used by social media platforms to display a preview of your website when it is shared. They include tags for title, description, image, and URL. By using Open Graph tags, you can control how your content appears on social media.

Twitter Cards: Similar to Open Graph tags, Twitter Cards allow you to control how your website appears on Twitter. They come in several formats, including summary, summary with large image, and app card. Choose the format that best suits your content.

Staying updated with industry trends is crucial to adapting your meta tag strategy for continued SEO success. Keep an eye out for updates to search engine algorithms and changes in user behavior to ensure that your website remains visible and relevant.

CSS FOR STYLING HTML

Introduction to CSS

CSS, or Cascading Style Sheets, is a crucial element in web development, serving as a powerful styling language meticulously crafted to enhance the presentation and layout aspects of HTML documents. This dynamic framework empowers developers to choreograph the visual rendering of elements on a webpage, embodying the separation of concerns paradigm.

What is CSS?

CSS defines the style and layout of multiple web pages simultaneously. It includes rules specifying how elements should be displayed, such as colors, fonts, spacing, and positioning. With CSS, you can create a consistent and visually appealing look for your website.

The Role of CSS:

CSS functions as the stylistic architect of a webpage, shaping how users perceive and interact with content. It provides developers with a comprehensive toolkit for defining visual properties, including colors, fonts, spacing, and positioning, ensuring coherence and consistency across multiple web pages.

Defining Styles and Layouts:

At its core, CSS involves formulating rules that dictate the appearance of HTML elements. These rules, executed through selectors and declarations, serve as blueprints for design implementation. Selectors identify HTML elements for styling, while declarations encapsulate specific stylistic directives, allowing developers to create intricate designs beyond HTML's limitations.

Separation of Content and Design:

CSS introduces an organizational paradigm that separates responsibilities in webpage creation. HTML focuses on content exposition, dictating structure and substance, while CSS, akin to a costume and set designer, refines visual aesthetics. This separation streamlines workflow, enabling content creators to focus on structure, and designers on aesthetics.

In the interplay of HTML and CSS, a harmonious synthesis unfolds, producing web pages that are structurally sound, visually captivating, and user-centric in professional web development.

Achieving Consistency and Appeal:
CSS serves as the style guide for a website, establishing rules for a cohesive look. Developers use CSS to ensure consistency across all pages, creating a neat and organized appearance. Consistency, like wearing a team jersey, fosters a sense of unity and is beneficial for branding. Visitors benefit from a predictable and navigable experience, as CSS unifies the website's visual elements.

In simple terms, CSS contributes to making all pages on a website visually cohesive, enhancing the overall user experience.

Inline, Internal, and External CSS:

Inline CSS:
Inline CSS is applied directly to an HTML element using the style attribute. It's useful for applying unique styles to a specific element.

Example:
This is a paragraph with inline CSS.

Internal (Embedded) CSS:
Internal or embedded CSS is placed within the <style> element in the <head> section of an HTML document. It applies styles to specific elements on that page.

```
Example:
<head>
    <style>
        h1 {
                color: green;
                font-size: 24px;
        }
        p {
                color: purple;
                font-size: 16px;
        }
    </style>
</head>
<body>
    <h1>This is a heading</h1>
    <p>This is a paragraph with internal CSS.</p>
</body>
```

Internal and External CSS are both useful ways to style your website. While Internal CSS is defined within the head section of an HTML document using the style tag and applies styles to multiple elements within a single web page, External CSS is defined in a separate CSS file and linked to HTML documents using the link tag. This allows developers to apply styles to multiple web pages, ensuring consistency across the entire website.

Here are some additional points to consider when choosing between Internal and External CSS:
Internal CSS: It's more efficient than inline CSS, as it allows developers to apply styles to multiple elements within a single web page. It's easier to manage than inline CSS, as developers can make changes to styles in one place rather than searching for inline styles throughout the HTML document.
It can still be used alongside External CSS, as it's possible to define both internal and external styles for the same element.

External CSS:
External CSS is stored in a separate file with a .css extension and linked to multiple HTML documents. This promotes consistency across the entire website.

It's easier to maintain than inline CSS, as developers can make changes to styles in one place and have those changes reflected across the entire website. It's more modular than inline CSS, as developers can create separate CSS files for different parts of the website (e.g. navigation, footer, etc.)

In the provided example, there is an inline CSS style applied to a paragraph element. While inline CSS can be useful for quickly applying styles to individual elements, it's generally not recommended for larger websites as it can be difficult to manage and maintain. Instead, using Internal or External CSS is a better option for larger websites with numerous pages.

```
styles.css:
h1 {
    color: red;
    font-size: 28px;
}
p {
    color: #333;
    font-size: 18px;
}
```

```
index.html:
<head>
    <link rel="stylesheet" type="text/css" href="styles.css">
</head>
<body>
    <h1>This is a heading</h1>
    <p>This is a paragraph with external CSS.</p>
</body>
```

Understanding the basics of CSS and its application methods—inline, internal, and external—empowers you to create visually appealing and consistent web designs. Whether you need styles for a specific element or want to maintain a unified look across multiple pages, CSS is a powerful tool for front-end development.

CSS Selectors
CSS selectors, covering understanding selectors, class and ID selectors, and the concepts of grouping and specificity.

Understanding Selectors
CSS selectors are patterns that define which elements in an HTML document will be styled by the associated rules. Selectors target HTML elements based on their type, attributes, relationships with other elements, and more. They play a crucial role in specifying the scope of styles to be applied.

Examples of Basic Selectors:

```
Element Selector:
p {
  color: blue;
```

```
}
```

This targets all <p> elements in the document.

ID Selector:

```
#header {
  background-color: gray;
}
```

This targets the element with the ID "header."

Class Selector:

```
.highlight {
  font-weight: bold;
}
```

This targets all elements with the class "highlight." This targets all elements with the class "highlight."

The class selector in CSS is a powerful tool that allows developers to select and style a group of elements with a single identifier. In the provided code, the class selector ".highlight" is used to target all elements that have the class "highlight". To style the selected elements, the code uses the "font-weight" property to make the text bold. This is just one example of how the class selector can be used to style elements.

To add a class to an element, use the "class" attribute in the HTML code.

For example, <p class="highlight">This text will be bold.</p> will apply the "highlight" class to the paragraph element.

Multiple classes can be applied to the same element by separating them with a space.
For example, <p class="highlight text red">This text will be bold and red.</p> will apply both the "highlight" and "text-red" classes to the paragraph element.

The order in which classes are listed in the "class" attribute does not matter, as long as they are separated by spaces. When defining styles for a class selector, you can include any valid CSS property, such as font-size, color, background-color, padding, margin, and more.

It's good practice to choose class names that are descriptive and easy to remember. This will make it easier to apply the same styles to multiple elements throughout your website. When using the class selector, keep in mind that it selects elements based on their class attribute, not their tag name or ID. This means that multiple elements can have the same class and be styled in the same way, regardless of their tag name.

Class and ID Selectors:

- Class Selector:
Classes are used to style multiple elements that share a common characteristic. To apply a class, use a period followed by the class name.

```
<p class="highlight">This is a highlighted paragraph.</p>
```

```
.highlight {
```

```
  color: red;
}
```

ID Selector:

IDs are used to uniquely style a specific element on the page. To apply an ID, use a hash followed by the ID name.

This targets the element with the ID "header."

The ID selector is a powerful tool in CSS that allows developers to style individual elements with a unique identifier. In the provided code, we can see that the ID "header" is being targeted and styled with a gray background color.

Here are some additional points to consider with ID selectors:

IDs are unique: Unlike classes, which can be applied to multiple elements, IDs must be unique to a single element. This means that only one element on the page should have a given ID. ID selectors start with a hash symbol (#): When targeting an element with an ID, the selector should begin with a hash symbol followed by the ID name. IDs are useful for targeting specific elements: If you have an element on the page that needs to be styled in a very specific way, using an ID selector can be a good choice.

For example, if you have a navigation bar at the top of your page and you want to style it differently than the rest of the content, you could give it an ID of "nav" and then target it with CSS. Be careful not to overuse IDs: While IDs can be useful, it's important not to rely on them too heavily. If you find yourself using IDs to style every element on the page, you may be better off using classes or other selectors instead.

Overall, the ID selector is a powerful tool that can be very useful when used correctly. Just remember to use it sparingly and only when necessary to avoid cluttering your CSS code.

```
<div id="main-content">Main Content Goes Here</div>
```

```
#main-content {
  font-size: 18px;
}
```

Note: While IDs should be unique on a page, classes can be applied to multiple elements.

Grouping and Specificity:
- Grouping Selectors:
You can group multiple selectors together to apply the same styles to different elements.

```
h1, h2, h3 {
  color: purple;
}
```

This applies the specified color to all <h1>, <h2>, and <h3> elements.

- Specificity:
Specificity is a measure of how the browser decides which CSS rule to apply when there are

conflicting styles. It's determined by the combination of selectors used.

Example:

```
/* Higher Specificity */
#main-content {
  color: red;
}

/* Lower Specificity */
p {
  color: blue;
}
```

In this example, the #main-content selector has higher specificity than the p selector, so its styles will take precedence.

Understanding and mastering CSS selectors is essential for effective styling and layout control in web development. It allows developers to precisely target and style specific elements, making the presentation of web content visually appealing and cohesive.

CSS Box Model
The CSS Box Model is a fundamental concept that describes how elements are structured and spaced within a webpage. It consists of margins, padding, borders, and the content area.

Margins, Padding, and Borders:
Content Area: This is where the actual content of the element, such as text or images, is displayed.

Padding: The padding is the space between the content and the element's border. It adds internal space within the box.

```
.box {
  padding: 20px;
}
```

Border: The border surrounds the padding, and it is the outermost visible edge of the box.

```
.box {
  border: 2px solid #000;
}
```

Margin: The margin is the space outside the border. It provides spacing between the border of one element and the adjacent elements.

```
.box {
  margin: 10px;
}
```

Box Sizing:
The box-sizing property determines how the total width and height of an element are calculated.

The default value is content-box, which only includes the content area. Alternatively, you can use border-box, which includes padding and border in the total width and height.

```
.box {
  box-sizing: border-box;}
```

CSS Units (px, em, rem, %):
Pixels (px): A fixed unit that provides a precise size.

```
.box {
  width: 200px;
}
```

Em (em): Relative to the font-size of the nearest parent element.

```
.box {
  font-size: 16px; /* Parent font-size */
  padding: 1em; /* Equals 16px */
}
```

Rem (rem): Relative to the font-size of the root element (typically <html>).

```
html {
  font-size: 16px; /* Root font-size */
}
```

```
.box {
  padding: 2rem; /* Equals 32px */
}
```

Percentage (%): Relative to the parent element's property.

```
.parent {
  width: 300px;
}
```

```
.child {
  width: 50%; /* Equals 150px */
}
```

Understanding and manipulating the CSS Box Model, along with the appropriate use of units, is crucial for creating responsive and visually appealing layouts. It gives developers precise control over the spacing and dimensions of elements on a webpage.

CSS Flexbox and Grid

Layout with Flexbox:
Definition: Flexbox is a one-dimensional layout system for distributing space along a single axis —either horizontally or vertically. Flexbox, or the Flexible Box Layout, is a one-dimensional layout method for laying out items in rows or columns. It provides a more efficient and predictable way to

distribute space and align content, even when the size of items is unknown or dynamic.

Use Cases:
The use cases of CSS Flexbox, particularly its suitability for organizing items in a row or column, such as navigation menus or lists.

Use Cases for CSS Flexbox:

Navigation Menus:
- Scenario: When designing navigation bars or menus, where menu items need to be horizontally aligned.
- Flexbox Property: `flex-direction: row;`
- Benefit: Ensures a clean and horizontal alignment of menu items, adapting easily to different screen sizes.

Css Code
```
.nav-menu {
  display: flex;
  flex-direction: row;
  justify-content: space-between;
}
```

Vertical Lists:
- Scenario: Creating vertical lists of items, such as a list of features or product details.
- Flexbox Property: `flex-direction: column;`
- Benefit: Allows easy vertical stacking of items, providing a neat and structured presentation.

Css Code:
```
.vertical-list {
  display: flex;
  flex-direction: column;
}
```

Card Layouts:
- Scenario: Designing card-based layouts where cards need to be arranged in a row or column.
- Flexbox Property: Depends on the desired orientation (`row` or `column`).
- Benefit: Flexbox simplifies the arrangement of cards with consistent spacing and alignment.

Css Code
```
.card-container {
  display: flex;
  flex-direction: row; /* or column */
  justify-content: space-between;
}
```

Media Objects:
- Scenario: Arranging media elements like images with associated text.
- Benefit: Flexbox ensures proper alignment of media elements, allowing for a flexible and responsive layout.

Css Code
```
.media-object {
  display: flex;
  align-items: center;
}
```

Footer Layouts:
- Scenario: Designing footers with multiple sections like links, social icons, and copyright information.
- Flexbox Property: Depends on the desired arrangement (e.g., `row`, `column`).
- Benefit: Flexbox simplifies the alignment of footer elements with consistent spacing.

```
.footer {
  display: flex;
  flex-direction: row;
  justify-content: space-between;
}
```

In summary, CSS Flexbox is particularly effective in scenarios where items need to be organized in a row or column. Its versatility and simplicity make it well-suited for creating responsive and aesthetically pleasing layouts in various web design components, including navigation menus, lists, card layouts, media objects, and footers.

Container Property: display: flex; or display: inline-flex;

Properties for Container (Parent):
- display: flex;` or `display: inline-flex;
  - Defines a flex container.
  - `flex` enables a block-level container, while `inline-flex` enables an inline-level container.

  - flex-direction:
  - Defines the main axis of the flex container.
  - Values: `row`, `row-reverse`, `column`, `column-reverse`.

- justify-content:
  - Aligns items along the main axis.
  - Values: `flex-start`, `flex-end`, `center`, `space-between`, `space-around`, `space-evenly`.

  - align-items:
  - Aligns items along the cross axis.
  - Values: `stretch`, `flex-start`, `flex-end`, `center`, `baseline`.

- align-self:
  - Allows the default alignment to be overridden for individual flex items.

Properties for Items (Children):
  - flex-grow:
  - Defines the ability for a flex item to grow.
  - Default value is 0; it won't grow.

- flex-shrink:
    - Defines the ability for a flex item to shrink.
    - Default value is 1.

- flex-basis:
    - Defines the initial size of a flex item.

order:
    - Controls the order in which the flex items appear in the flex container.

Example:
```
.container {
  display: flex;
  flex-direction: row;
  justify-content: space-between;
  align-items: center;
}

.item {
  flex-grow: 1;
}
```

CSS Grid:
CSS Grid Layout is a two-dimensional layout system for the web. It lets you layout items into rows and columns, creating complex grid structures with ease.

Properties for Container (Parent):
    - display: grid:
        - Defines a grid container.

    - grid-template-rows` and `grid-template-columns:
        - Specifies the size of rows and columns in the grid.

    - grid-template-areas:
        - Defines named grid areas in the layout.

    - grid-gap` or `grid-row-gap` and `grid-column-gap:
        - Sets the gap between rows and/or columns.

    - justify-items` and `align-items:
        - Aligns grid items in the grid container.

Properties for Items (Children):
    - grid-row` and `grid-column:
        - Specifies on which row or column the item should be placed.

    - grid-area:
        - Assigns the item to a named grid area.

    - justify-self` and `align-self:

- Aligns a grid item inside a cell along the inline (row) or block (column) axis.

Example:

Css code:
```
.container {
  display: grid;
  grid-template-columns: 1fr 2fr 1fr;
  grid-template-rows: auto;
  grid-gap: 10px;
}

.item {
  grid-column: 2 / 3;
  grid-row: 1;
}
```

Layout with Flexbox:

Flexbox is great for one-dimensional layouts, such as navigation bars or lists, where items flow in a single direction.

Creating Grids with CSS Grid:
CSS Grid is powerful for two-dimensional layouts, like complex grid structures for entire page layouts, with rows and columns working together.

In practice, both Flexbox and Grid are often used in combination to achieve sophisticated and responsive layouts, taking advantage of the strengths of each layout system.

Semantic HTML is a way of writing HTML that emphasizes the meaning of the content rather than its presentation. Semantic HTML uses specific tags to describe the content of a web page, making it easier for search engines and screen readers to understand the structure of the page. Here's a brief overview of some of the most commonly used semantic elements:

- Header: The <header> element is used to define a header section for a document or a section. It usually contains a logo, navigation menu, and other introductory content.
- Nav: The <nav> element is used to define a section of navigation links.
- Article: The <article> element is used to define an independent, self-contained piece of content, such as a blog post or news article.
- Section: The <section> element is used to define a section of related content.
- Footer: The <footer> element is used to define a footer section for a document or a section. It usually contains copyright information, contact details, and other closing content.

Here's an example of semantic HTML:
```
<header>
 <h1>My Website</h1>
 <nav>
  <ul>
```

```
        <li><a href="#">Home</a></li>
        <li><a href="#">About</a></li>
        <li><a href="#">Contact</a></li>
      </ul>
    </nav>
  </header>

  <main>
    <article>
      <h2>Article Title</h2>
      <p>Article content goes here...</p>
    </article>

    <section>
      <h2>Section Title</h2>
      <p>Section content goes here...</p>
    </section>
    <aside>
      <h2>Aside Title</h2>
      <p>Aside content goes here...</p>
    </aside>
    <footer>
      <p>&copy; My Website 2023</p>
    </footer>
  </main>
```

In this example, we have used semantic HTML elements to define the structure of a web page. The <header> element contains the site's logo and navigation menu, while the <main> element contains the main content of the page. The <article> element contains an independent piece of content, while the <section> element contains a section of related content. The <aside> element contains content that is related to the main content but not essential to it, and the <footer> element contains closing content such as copyright information.

Difference between div and section tag in HTML5

```
<header>
  <h1>My Website</h1>
  <nav>
    <ul>
      <li><a href="#">Home</a></li>
      <li><a href="#">About</a></li>
      <li><a href="#">Contact</a></li>
    </ul>
  </nav>
</header>

<main>
```

```
<article>
  <h2>Article Title</h2>
  <p>Article content goes here...</p>
</article>

<section>
  <h2>Section Title</h2>
  <p>Section content goes here...</p>
</section>

<aside>
  <h2>Aside Title</h2>
  <p>Aside content goes here...</p>
</aside>

<footer>
  <p>© My Website 2023</p>
</footer>
</main>
```

In this example, we have used semantic HTML elements to define the structure of a web page. The <header> element contains the site's logo and navigation menu, while the <main> element contains the main content of the page. The <article> element contains an independent piece of content, while the <section> element contains a section of related content. The <aside> element contains content that is related to the main content but not essential to it, and the <footer> element contains closing content such as copyright information.

CONCLUSION

Congratulations on completing this journey through the world of web development and design! We've covered a range of topics, from laying the foundation with Semantic HTML to organizing data using HTML Tables. We delved into the intricacies of creating advanced forms with HTML and explored the crucial realm of SEO through HTML Meta Tags. Finally, we put the cherry on top by understanding how to style our HTML using CSS.

By now, you should have a solid understanding of the fundamental building blocks of web development. Remember that Semantic HTML not only structures your content but also enhances accessibility and SEO. Tables are powerful tools for presenting data in a clear and organized manner, while advanced forms provide a dynamic and interactive user experience. The knowledge of HTML Meta Tags ensures that your content is not just visible but also discoverable on the vast landscape of the internet.

And let's not forget the aesthetics—CSS is the artist's palette, allowing you to breathe life into your HTML, making it visually appealing and engaging for your audience.

As you move forward in your web development journey, keep experimenting, building, and refining your skills. The web is ever-evolving, and staying curious and adaptable will be your greatest assets. Whether you're creating a personal blog, an e-commerce site, or the next big web application, the principles you've learned here will serve as a strong foundation.

Don't miss out on the opportunity to unlock the potential of web development. Grab your copy here and let "Mastering HTML" be your companion on your coding adventures. As you close this digital chapter, remember that the web is waiting for your creative contributions. Happy coding!